HOW TO BE OUTSTANDING AT WORK

Organization, Communication, Problem Solving and Continuous Learning

Camila Carvalho

Copyright © 2022 Camila Carvalho

All rights reserved

No part of this book may be reproduced, or stored in a retrieval system, or transmitted in any form or by any means, electronic, mechanical, photocopying, recording, or otherwise, without express written permission of the publisher.

ASIN : B0B39N134Z
ISBN-13 : 979-8830024396

INTRODUCTION

Are you a young person at the beginning of your **career** and you're not sure about how to direct your efforts to progress? Do you have trouble getting **organized** as you are always suffocated by everyday's tasks? Are you unsure about how is the best way to **communicate** with your colleagues? Are you nervous just by thinking about the **problems** you will encounter at work?

In this book, you'll find helpful tips on how to overcome these obstacles and become a professional everyone wants to work with. Here is a summary of the next chapters:

1) **Organization**: How to manage your time and prioritize your tasks.

2) **Communication**: After all, you need to communicate well regardless of the type of work you do.

3) **Problem Solving**: You were hired because your company expects you to be able to find out solutions to its

problems. But is that what you're doing?

4) **Development of skills and abilities**: Do you think that if you wait patiently, the company will recognize you are a good professional and it will give you a promotion, like that, out of the blue? Or do you think you should show them how good you are? In the final chapter, you'll see how you can obtain the skills and abilities you need to thrive in your career.

Let's start by understanding why organization is one of the most important skills you should have in your job.

1- ORGANIZATION

The art of procrastinating

Let's start by talking about procrastination, which is the act of putting off a situation to be solved **later**. And, as you may already know, it is extremely common in the workplace.

Usually, we have something very **important** to do and we put it off as much as possible. And to be a good professional, it is imperative that we deliver what we are being paid to do. Or would you hire someone who never completes anything and just wastes the company's time?

Procrastinating is something everyone does to a greater or lesser extent. But why do we procrastinate so much? Why don't we just do the things we have to do? You have already experienced this feeling. When you're at work and you have an important task, the hours drag on and you can't even take the first step. Something always pops up to grab your attention.

Here are three reasons why you might be procrastinating on your tasks:

1. **Fear of failure**. Often, we do not start an activity for fearing not being able to perform it correctly. Also, we could be unsure about the activity itself (if it's the right thing to do at the moment). Or even, we could be afraid of reworks. So, we decide to do everything at the last minute to use it as an excuse of why the quality of our work is not as good as expected.

By the way, this is not a character flaw. This is a result of a culture that teaches us from an early age that failure is wrong. We keep hoping to get everything right from the very first time. We end up being unable to start anything because of this perfectionism.

2. **Fear of commitment**. That's when we do self-sabotage. You wait as long as possible and then do everything at once in a very clumsy way, already knowing you are not delivering a good service and then someone else needs to fix what you did.

So, next time the company needs that service again, they certainly won't ask you to do it, because you can't be trusted. In the short term, you'll be free of the commitment, but this will end up being bad for your reputation, as your colleagues and your boss won't trust you and you'll compromise your future at the company.

3. **Fear of success**. We procrastinate, even knowing we could do a better job if we used all the time available, instead of leaving everything to the last minute. Many times, we get disappointed for not feeling recognized for a well done task. And then, we think there's no point in being efficient if there's no reward for it.

Also, sometimes you do a well done job and you think they will start demanding that level of quality from now on. But getting new responsibilities is not bad at all, it means you are evolving and that soon, you'll be able to take on more responsibilities in the future and progress in your career.

However, it is natural to be afraid, because all progress involves change. And we are naturally afraid of change, because no matter how bad something is, we are used to our current situation. But don't be limited by this kind of thinking. After all, you can be much more successful than you are today.

Okay, now you know some reasons for procrastination. But how do you deal with it? If you can't start something, the tip is simple. So simple you won't believe it:

Just get it started.

Don't expect to be **motivated**. We are used to think we need to wait for some kind of **inspiration** to strike in order to accomplish something, but it can be just the opposite. If you need to do something and you don't know where to start, the best thing you can do is to **start** anyway.

If you have a report to write, start by typing a few loose sentences, but keep in mind this will not be the final version of the document. As soon as you start, you will see there is already something ready in your head, but it will not necessarily be the introduction of that report. Do the middle, the end and then the beginning if you have to. Keep changing the parts you didn't like. **Review** until satisfied. At first glance, it may sound like **rework**, but it's not. In fact, you will be creating an initial version that will improve and evolve until it is at a quality standard that you are comfortable with.

It's much better to do it that way, because you can give your creativity a boost. When you read what you've written, your critical sense will feel the urge to correct what's not good and you'll feel much more excited to continue the work, because you'll see some progress in the activity.

And this feeling is so much better than standing still, looking at the ceiling, and waiting for inspiration to hit.

Try doing this. You will feel much lighter and **motivated**.

Next, let's do a little **assignment** to think about what we're procrastinating at the moment. And then we'll talk about the difference between **important** and **urgent** tasks.

Assignment: What am I procrastinating?

Is there an activity or project you should be doing at work (or even in your personal life) that you can't even begin? Which one?

***

In addition to identifying what you're procrastinating on, it's important to find out the reason why you're putting off what you need to do.

Is it fear of: failure, success or commitment?

Think about it and then try to start it at once, planning your steps first. Break the activity down into smaller parts so you won't feel intimidated by the size of the work. By doing it in stages, you will be able to visualize your progress.

Important x Urgent

We tend to focus more on "putting out fires" than on performing the tasks that are really **important** and that make a difference in the long run. It's easier to get busy with the little things that seemingly have to be dealt with at the moment, while forgetting to take the time to deal with items that won't have an **immediate** negative impact, but will need to be done sooner or later. We leave aside the more **complex** activities because we know they will take more **time** to do. But eventually we'll have to deal with them. Meanwhile, we get anxious and, consequently, more exhausted.

One factor that contributes to this problem is we often don't know how to distinguish what is **important** from what is **urgent**. To improve your perception, try to prioritize your activities taking into account the possible **consequences** if they are not carried out. That is, when choosing what you will prefer to do first, think about the following:

What would happen if activity A were not done? What about activity B?

Now, compare their possible consequences. The one with the most serious consequence should be prioritized. Just be careful, as to not make mistakes when prioritizing. That's why it's also interesting to stop from time to time to reflect on the very nature of your activities. Sometimes, we are so used to performing a certain activity in a certain way that we don't stop to think if there is better way to do it.

Also note that this is an effect of our **culture**. When we took a test at school, for example, it was recommended that we answered the easiest questions first and left the most difficult ones to the end. This got us used to postponing more complex tasks due to an alleged lack of time. But in professional life, we can't stop doing our tasks by using this kind of excuse. If your time is really scarce, then you need to choose the activities that add most value to the company. Unfortunately, we tend to choose the **easiest** and **immediate** tasks.

So, try to set aside a period at the beginning of the day just for the most important and complex activities, which require greater concentration. In this way, you will have a more rested mind to be able to work with greater tranquility and even more creatively. Leave the rest of the day to do more **mechanical** activities, which don't require a lot of thinking, but have to be done anyway.

Managing your time

If you have **autonomy** to manage your routine at work,

it is likely that sometimes you feel your time isn't enough. If you are one of those people who use an planner, even so you may still not be able to fulfill everything you have to do and can be frustrated at the end of the day. On the other hand, if you don't even have the habit of **planning,** it can be even harder to complete your activities. Your routine might be very stressful and it only gets worse when you don't have a minimum of organization. And what can you do about it?

First, you need to choose a tool to list your daily activities and write it down when you complete them. It can be a notebook, a planner, an app or even a spreadsheet. But it has to be something convenient for you. For example, it's no use adopting a notebook if you work standing up most of the day and have to carry that weight back and forth. It also doesn't work to install an app if your company doesn't allow the use of smartphones during working hours.

However, if you work all day using your computer, you could use a spreadsheet while doing your job. The important thing is that you use any of these tools, as long as it is in line with your reality. That's because your brain was made to **process** information and not to remember things. If you have to do both, you will do neither. It is a waste of your mental capacity. So, if you have any prejudice with a planner, it's time to change.

Here are some tips on how to get better organized:

Make a **weekly schedule**. You can prepare it on the Friday of the previous week and when Monday arrives, you just review it to check if you are going to include or exclude any items that day. It's important to get the whole week organized, rather than planning just one day at a time. This will give you a good view of what you have to accomplish in the next few days and if things change, you can make **adjustments**.

Also, remember to prioritize. We've just talked about important and urgent activities. Always try to do the important activities earlier in the morning to make sure your brain is well rested. And don't fill up your day with too many activities. Put in a good amount of tasks, but leave room for unforeseen, because something you weren't expecting can suddenly need your attention. It can be a phone call, an unplanned meeting and all sorts of things.

As a rule, think of filling your schedule as if you were only going to work **half** your shift. If, for example, you work 8 hours a day, put in activities you estimate will take a maximum of 4 hours to complete. This will give you a break in case an activity goes on longer than planned and you need more time. In addition, you will be able to deal with the problems that arise, without it affecting your schedule.

Finally, you should alternate between easy and difficult activities. What I mean is that if you're doing an important and complex activity from 8:00 to 9:00, by 9:00 do something more mechanical. Then go back to the previous activity. This will give you some relaxation, but without that feeling of guilt for thinking you're stalling at work.

It is important to intersperse activities, because when people manage to get into a flow and spend hours working on something very difficult, they are so exhausted afterwards that they can't work on anything else. Result: they go out for a coffee and only resume the activity the next day. So, whenever you feel your head starting to heat up, switch to something more relaxed and then get back on track, okay?

And one more thing: **record** that you completed the activity. Whether crossing it off on the planner or putting a bookmark next to it. It sounds silly, but it serves as a small **reward** and makes you feel more **motivated** to keep working.

Summing up

In this chapter, we saw three reasons why we

procrastinate: fear of **failure**, fear of **commitment**, and fear of **success**.

We've seen that if you need to do something and you don't know where to start, the best thing you can do is just start. **Action** can come before motivation. Take action and feel motivated.

We also saw that we need to distinguish between **important** and **urgent** activities, giving preference to performing the most important and complex activities early in the day.

Finally, we need to have our **weekly schedule** organized and prioritized, but leaving free time to deal with unforeseen events.

Now that you have an idea of how to better **organize** your work, let's see how you can improve your **communication** skills.

2 - COMMUNICATION

In this chapter, we'll start by talking about the communication methods we can use at work. Next, we'll talk about some mistakes you might be committing when communicating with your pairs. And finally, let's understand the importance of observing and listening.

Communication methods

To be a good communicator, you need to understand there are many ways to communicate. And each one of them has its usefulness according to the moment and according to the person you want to talk to. The most common means of communication nowadays are: Phone, Email, WhatsApp/Telegram and, of course, face to face.

There must be a relation between the **urgency** of the matter to be addressed and the means of communication to be used.

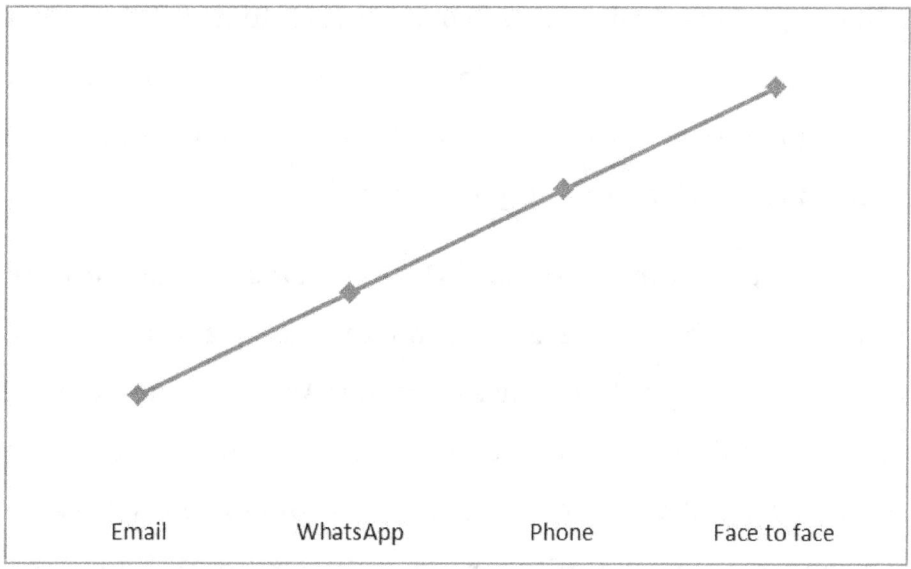

If, for example, there is a matter you need to deal with and it does not require an immediate response, or if you are just passing on information, then an email is more than enough. Also, email has the advantage of keeping a record of the conversation in case you need to come back to the subject in the future. In the same way, you can also communicate by letters, crafts, memos and others. All these means of communication are used when we need to deal with things formally.

However, if you are in a bit of a **hurry**, you can use WhatsApp. And when I say WhatsApp, it's because it's the most popular application on the market that performs this type of function nowadays. You may use others, such as: Telegram,

Discord, Slack, etc. Note that unlike email, you can talk via WhatsApp in real-time, whether you're sending text messages or audio messages. In addition, it also has the function of making audio or video calls. Therefore, you can communicate with your interlocutor as if you were on the phone.

Keep in mind that the **rules** for using this application shall be very clear. There are companies that approve it and companies that don't, because on WhatsApp, you can either be solving pending issues about your work or sending jokes in the family group. And the rules must apply to both sides, because we have to establish **limits** for the company too. You shouldn't be warned because you didn't see a message your boss sent you after your shift. Also, the use of WhatsApp forces people to always be connected. And when they are always connected, they lose productivity due to lack of concentration. So, it's a good communication tool and even more agile than email, but if we're not careful, it can contribute to increasing stress.

Next, we have the **phone** (and cellphones and calls in general). The phone is ideal for when we need an answer **right away**. However, try not to call people if the matter is not really important and urgent. In general, no one likes to be bothered with calls, but there are some situations only a phone call can solve.

Finally, we have the **face to face** communication. Talking to people is very important, mainly because nowadays we are very disconnected from each other. When the person is in front of you, you not only hear what they have to say, but you can catch the gestures they make, you can look them in the eye, and see things they are not saying with words. Whenever possible, prefer this form of communication, because it is easier to being understood and you can have a better connection with your interlocutor.

The problem is we often do not use the means of communication according to what the situation requires. Sometimes out of shame, sometimes because we don't really want to deal with the problem. It is now so common for us to communicate indirectly, through social media, that people are starting to feel intimidated when having to talk to someone face to face, however necessary it is. You may know someone who, for example, almost dies of **anxiety** just by hearing a phone ringing and who can't even call to make an appointment with the doctor. On the other hand, that same person may be able to express themselves very well through Facebook, Twitter and Instagram. But if they have to talk to someone on the phone, they panic.

So, what to do in that case? How do we overcome this

modern shyness? We'll cover that later in this chapter, but first, let's talk about what not to do when communicating with someone.

The wrong way to communicate

Establishing a good communicating solves a lot of problems. And in the same way, communicating poorly can make your life very difficult. There are several ways to commit communication **failures**. It's easier to get it wrong than right in this matter. So, here are **three mistakes** you can already avoid from now on.

First: write in a **clumsy way**. Spelling and grammar errors are problematic when they **compromise** the information we want to pass on. If it's hard enough to follow instructions when someone writes everything correctly, imagine when you can't even understand what the person meant. When we write well, we speak better. And nowadays, we have many ways to improve our English for **free**. You can: watch videos on YouTube, read blogs, magazines, and books. You can even study by smartphone apps.

A note: You can speak **informally** if the person you are dealing with also speaks informally to you. But if it's a formal communication, follow the rules, ok? It all depends on your interlocutor and the purpose of the message. This book, for example, favors a simpler and more informal language, as the objective is to facilitate the understanding of the message. But it would not be the right tone for a work report, for example.

Studying **grammar** and spelling can be very boring because the way we had to learn it at school. So, you can start your study by doing this Google search: *"What are the main English mistakes?"* You will find a series of articles, some with a very simple speech. It might be easier that way because you'll be curious to know if you make any of those mistakes, or if you've already mastered the items on the list.

Furthermore, when you have any doubts when writing a text, do not hesitate to check it out if you are writing it correctly. But you don't need to use unfamiliar words or fancy rules. Just communicate in a way your interlocutor can understand.

Okay and what else can go wrong with our communication?

Have you ever heard about **defensive posture**? When you try to reason with a person and they believe they are being attacked? They interrupt you, they don't listen to you and no matter what you do, they just care about being right. Well, everyone is guilty of having behaved like that at least once. Therefore, it is important you always seek to adopt a **learning posture** instead.

Understand that even if you believe you are right, you need to **hear** others people's thoughts because they can contribute to improve your initial idea. Don't cling to your **arguments** as if they were a part of you, because you will take everything as an offense. Have humility. Winning an argument doesn't make you better than anyone else, especially if you win by force. When you forcefully win an argument, no one really does what you say because they were convinced by you. People do what you want because they're **tired** of arguing. So, when arguing, think about the problem you want to solve **together** and not about winning a trophy for being the "master" of the discussion.

Another problem that happens in all companies is **gossip**. And it's no use hiding because I know you've already gossiped. Everyone, without exception, has done it. But from now on, let's hold our tongue. And do you know why? Gossip doesn't benefit the work environment at all. It only helps to increase people's **insecurity** and create **animosity**. If you have something to say, or any questions about the company's situation, talk to the person in charge of the information. Don't talk about people behind their backs, no matter how much you feel that impulse of socialize with your colleagues. If you're in a room and people start to gossip, say them you don't think that's right and if you don't have the guts to say it, just get up and leave. I know it's really hard to resist gossip, because we love to hear stories. However, if you think about it, you'll realize that nothing good will ever come from it.

There are many **errors** that can compromise communication, in addition to those already mentioned here. So, always be aware of your behavior when interacting with people.

Observe and listen

Do you know why the title of this section is not **look** and **hear**? Because these words only refer to our senses and to what our eyes and ears can capture. However, you may be looking and hearing something without actually **observing** and **listening** to it.

To observe is to look at something carefully. It's really perceiving something, just as listening is understanding what is being picked up by hearing, and being able to process that information. To be able to establish good communication, you need to be **present**. And I'm not talking about a physical presence, but you need to be available for your interlocutor. After all, it's no use accepting to talk to someone if you're just browsing at your cell phone for the whole conversation.

Being able to observe and to listen are skills you can use both in your work and in your personal life. It is important to keep your eyes and ears open. It is even more crucial than knowing how to speak well, since, in order to send a good message, it is necessary to understand what people expect from you. And for that, you need to learn how to listen to them.

Imagine, for example, that you have just started a new job. What should you do? First, **observe** the environment before giving any advice to the people who already work there.

As soon as people get into their new job, they start pointing out flaws, to show they're putting their best foot forward. But if you start full of **criticism** too soon, maybe people will think that since you are a newbie, you don't understand anything about the company yet (even if you were correct in your observations).

Take some time and observe people's behavior and what the culture of the place is like. There is no deadline until you can issue opinions. In fact, it's not like you can't talk, but before you come up with solutions to problems that no one is seeing, ask **questions**. Show genuine interest in knowing what people think. If something seems strange or wrong to you, ask about it. If they don't give you a satisfactory answer, ask someone else. Your questions can make your coworkers wonder about the issue too.

When you talk to someone, really pay attention to what the person has to say. Watch their **gestures**, their posture; see if there's anything they're not saying in words. Be careful, it's very easy to think that what we have to say is more important than what others have to say. Ever notice that sometimes it feels like we're in a competition to see who talks the most and no one is really paying attention to anyone? The truth is people love to talk when they find a good listener and that goes for us too. So give the opportunity for others to be heard and appreciated too.

And for **shy people**, who can't even answer the phone without being paralyzed by fear, this can be a great tactic for dealing with shyness. You don't have to worry so much about talking if you're willing to **listen**. The problem is that shy people are afraid of even an initial contact. They tense up wondering if they will have something to talk about with someone they don't know, or if an awkward silence will prevail. On the other hand, when they open up for someone to approach, these same shy people become extremely **talkative**. In other words, they just need to feel comfortable in a safe environment.

But how to feel safe talking to mere acquaintances? How to address coworkers who pass by you every day? Here's another very simple tip. Whenever you pass by people, **greet them first**. Don't wait to see if they'll say good morning to respond to it. This kind of tension is a part of shy people's lives. So don't live in that suffering, in that expectation. When you're walking by the person, say good morning loud and clear and with a huge smile on your face. Give them a truly smile, so the person knows you really are wishing them a good day. Take this test when you're at work. You'll be surprised at how many serious expressions you can disarm with your smile.

Okay, what if you're not walking but sitting next to the person and you're afraid to say hello because you don't know what to say next? Don't worry, say good morning and if the person is talkative they will bring up a subject. And if they're talking about something you don't know well, don't worry, just listen until you feel conformable to give your opinion, or even ask questions to find out about it. People love to teach things.

Once the tension of the first contact wears off, you will be able to relax and communicate normally.

What if you say good morning and the person doesn't say anything? No problem, go mind your own business. But just the fact that you cracked a smile might have made them more likely to talk to you later. Be patient, after all, you might be dealing with someone as shy as you are.

Summing up

We talked about the main communication methods we can use at work and the relationship between the urgency of the matter and the means of communication to be used.

We saw some of the problems that can compromise good communication, such as: English mistakes, defensive posture and gossip at work.

Finally, we talked about the importance of observe, listen and show interest in what our interlocutor has to say.

Now that you have an idea of how to communicate better, let's see how we can become good problem solvers. This is a highly valued skill in any job.

3 – PROBLEM SOLVING

In this chapter, we'll see the different types of reaction when facing a problem. There are at least five ways to react according to your profile.

The 5 Problem Reaction Profiles

Problems are part of our life and they can cause us a lot of **anxiety**. To learn how to deal with them, we need to understand how is our typical response to them. The same problem can be looked at in different ways according to the **perspective** of the person trying to solve it. There are at least five profiles: The Denier, the Blame Hunter, the Martyr, the Pointer, and the Problem Solver. Let's see each one of them.

The Denier

This profile denies the very existence of a problem or deliberately omits it. He will try his best to sweep the situation under the rug. And if it gets discovered, he'll pretend he didn't know anything about it or that someone else was the real responsible.

If you fit this profile, realize that it's much less stressful to deal with a problem right away before it grows up. The problem won't just disappear, no matter how much you hope for it. If it's something you find too challenging, don't be shy about asking for help. After all, no one is born knowing how to do everything by themself, right?

The Blame Hunter

This one may even admit the existence of a problem, but is looking for **culprits** instead of solutions. And who doesn't know someone like that? The Blame Hunter thinks that by naming someone responsible, the problem will no longer have anything to do with him. But he doesn't realize once the situation has been created, it doesn't matter whose fault it is, the important is that it needs to be solved.

If you fit in that profile, try to **empathize** with people. Most of the time, no one will make a mistake because they wanted to, but because of lack of experience, or failure to communicate. So that person may already be feeling very bad and you will only make the situation worse by pointing the finger at them. Instead, collaborate to promote a **solution**, even if it's not your direct responsibility or even if it's a problem that happened in other sector of the company. If there's anything you can do to help, then do it gladly. Remember: the company needs all its sectors to be functioning well and not just yours.

The Martyr

The Martyr is that kind of person who takes all the blame to himself, but who can't take the initiative to actually solve anything. Also, martyrs don't delegate, they don't ask for help, they just **worry** but don't take any action. Sometimes they even ask for help, but only when it is too late.

If you identify with this profile, try to see things with a little more objectivity. Not every problem is the end of the world. Try to stop for a few minutes to think of a solution. And if it's something too complicated to solve by yourself, ask for help. Perhaps you just need some **guidance**.

The Pointer

The Pointer is very good at **identifying problems** and forwarding them to his superior. However, this only solves part of the situation as he leaves to his boss the responsibility of having to think about how to solve the problem he identified.

If you fit that profile, that's a good thing because you're already halfway to becoming a Problem Solver.

The Problem Solver

The Problem Solver, in addition to showing the problem, points out possible solutions. Instead of just saying, *"We have a problem,"* he says, *"We have a problem, but I have an idea to solve it."* If you have autonomy to implement the most suitable solution by yourself, that's even better. This is the kind of professional all companies want to have. That's being **proactive**. In other words, don't wait for things to resolve themselves, don't push this burden on anyone and don't even take it on yourself. Act objectively, **analyze** the problem and find a solution. And if it's possible, solve it without even bother anyone else.

Be a Problem Solver

To be a Problem Solver, you need to learn how to **solve problems**. And the first step in solving a problem is discovering everything you can about it. It's no use trying to solve a situation if you have no idea what it's about. Usually, people accept a challenge without knowing much **information**, just to not appear ignorant to their bosses. We are always afraid of being judged. So, it's common not to ask when we have doubts out of shame. And if there's one thing I'm going to repeat until you internalize it, it's: Ask. **Always ask**.

You know in movies when something goes wrong? When a misunderstanding happens? Well, it was probably because someone didn't ask the questions they should have. Do not let it happen to you. Communication failures are very exhausting and cause **expenses** that could be avoided if people felt safer to speak in the work environment. So, again, the first step in solving a problem is: To know everything you can about it. And how are you going to do that? Asking. And also researching on your own, of course.

Just be careful to not spend too much time at this stage and end up getting lost. Assess how much planning a problem requires to be solved. Simpler things will take less research time and more complex things will take more time, ok? Once you understand the problem, you will think about possible solutions and the **consequences** of each one.

For example, imagine that you have a **customer** complaining at your store. First, you talk to him to understand why he is unhappy and then try to come up with a solution. The customer says he is not happy with the product he purchased, because when he got home he realized that it was not what he needed. But as he had to travel the next day, he didn't have time to come to the store within the stipulated return period. And then, you visualize the following possibilities:

1) You say the store is not under a legal obligation to receive that product back. Yes, you can simply tell the customer that it's not your fault and you can't do anything for them. The consequence of this solution is that he will be upset and probably won't buy from your store anymore.

2) You can also accept the product back and return the customer's money. However, this is a product that, after opening the packaging, it loses a lot of its market value, so you would need to sell it at a lower price. On the other hand, your

customer may be very grateful and he will buy again in the future or even recommend the store to relatives and friends.

3) Or, you can ask him to choose a cheaper item from the store, to compensate for the loss you will have for receiving back a product with the opened package.

I'm not going to point out any of these solutions as the best solution. These are not even all the possible solutions to this problem. Just understand that, in the end, it all depends on what you're willing to accept as a **consequence**.

In the first case, you don't return the money and keep your profit in the short term. But you might not be doing business with this customer again. In the second case, you choose to lose money now in anticipation of a future gain. And in the third, both you and the customer lose a little, since he will not be so happy for purchasing a product of lower value.

Therefore, every **solution** creates an **impact** that can be positive or negative. So remember to always be aware of the consequences of your decisions. This is the simplest way to solve problems.

Summing up

In this chapter, we saw we approach problems in different ways and there are at least five reaction profiles: The Denier, the Blame Hunter, the Martyr, the Pointer, and the Problem Solver.

We've seen that we need to become Problem Solvers and not mere Pointers. And how do we do that?

First, we try to **understand** everything we can about the situation and then we think about possible solutions to the problem. Remembering that each solution comes with a **consequence**.

Now that you know that to be a good professional you need to: be organized, to know how to communicate and to be a good **problem solver**, let's understand why it is important to develop skills and abilities to progress in your career.

4 - DEVELOPMENT OF SKILLS AND ABILITIES

In this chapter, you'll figure out if you're really in the right **profession** and what you can do if you want to change careers. In addition, we'll see why it is so important to continuously develop our **skills** and **abilities** and how we can combine our daily activities with our learning.

What do you want to be when you grow up?

Everyone must have heard that question as a child. But when we reach adulthood, we stop chasing what we **wanted** to be and we start to be what we **can** be, because we have bills to pay.

Many people have no idea why they work in a particular field. They started there for some reason and they stayed there, either because they settled down or because they didn't believe there were options available. And what was to be a **temporary** job ends up becoming a profession. Some even find fulfillment that way. Others, not so much.

Imagine that you started working in accounting at the age of eighteen because someone got you a job in that field. But you never really liked it, but continued because it helped you pay the **bills**. Also, you couldn't find enough time to study something else at the same time. And now you believe it's too late to change professions.

This could even have been the reality back in the day. When people graduated in an area and exercised that profession until the end of their lives. But today, we can't even afford to think we'll be doing the same thing twenty years from now. A lot can change and the only certainty is that we will need to be much more versatile than we are today. We are hardly going to work with just one specific thing, as it is today, so it is vital that you are already preparing to adapt to the **future**.

However, before you despair, let's think about what you can do to align the work you already do today with what you actually want to do in the future. Of course, there's no way to predict exactly what the world is going to be in twenty years from now, but if you're dissatisfied with your job, let's at least try to guide you to the area you have the most affinity, okay?

You need to ask yourself two questions:

- What kind of work I **do** in my company?
- What kind of work I **would like** to do?

You may find yourself in one of these three situations:

1) You are already happy with your current profession. This is the best of all worlds because all you need to worry about is staying current and relevant to the market.

2) You are not totally happy with what you do, but what you want to do is something that has some relation to your current job. For example, you may work in tax accounting, but you would prefer to work in the personnel department area. Or if you work with finance and realize you have an affinity for marketing. As much as these are different areas, you can use the **experience** you have and learn the skills and abilities missing to work in the area that you want. Instead of thinking this is a weakness, think about how cool it would be for a company to be able to hire a marketer who also has experience in finance. Maybe he would be capable to do a lot more with the money available for his advertising campaigns.

If you found yourself in this situation, you will need to go after what you lack to change your profession. Maybe you don't need to get another degree; maybe short-term technical courses would be enough. But you will likely have to spend time at your current job while you gain knowledge about your new area of expertise.

If the company you work for has vacancies available in the sector you want to work for, it is important you make your interest clear so you can be an option to be considered. Don't expect your company to guess what you want to be. Combine a plan with them and see if you can make this **transition**. And if not, get the necessary experience while looking for jobs that better suits you.

3) And finally, when you ask yourself those two questions at the beginning, you may discover that: what you want to be has nothing to do with what you do today. For example, you might be a lawyer who discovered that your dream is to be a physical therapist. This situation is similar to the previous one, but with the difference that a person who works in a law firm would hardly get a job as a physical therapist in that same workplace.

So, you would have to make a bigger effort to get a new degree, while staying in your current job until you can make this transition with peace of mind. But if that's your case, don't give up just because it's harder.

Either way, it's better than spending the rest of your life working on something that doesn't make you happy. And don't consider a profession you've abandoned as wasted time. All experience is valid and although you may not realize it, you can even use part of the learning you already have in your new profession.

And finally, here are some points you should pay attention to when deciding about what you want to do:

1) What you **want to be** versus what you **can be** at your company.

See if you can align your expectations with the company's expectations. After all, you may be dissatisfied with the work you are currently doing, but not necessarily with the company you work for.

2) Have a **Plan B**.

If where you work there is not much room for growth, you should monitor the emergence of possible vacancies in other companies. Try to find out about the size of the market. Is there a demand in your city for professionals in the area in which you want to work?

3) **Don't hit on everything that walks**. First of all, stay focused. Don't just send out resumes randomly. If by the end of the day you have decided you are really going to change companies, do a good research on your possible options and when a vacancy arises, try to really get to know what this company does and what its working environment is like.

It's not interesting to move to an environment that you don't fit in. Imagine you are a non-smoker and you receive an offer to work in a company that produces cigarettes, where people are allowed to smoke inside the workplace.

Understand that it's not just the company that chooses you; you must decide if it's the right place to work. When we discover the vacancy, it is normal to only think about the money involved, but keep in mind that money does bring happiness, but only if it is followed by good experiences.

Next, we'll see why it's important to develop our **skills** and **abilities**.

Why develop skills and abilities?

There are people who think that after obtaining a degree, they will no longer need to study. And unfortunately, that is not true. We always need to **improve** ourselves because the more we know, the more we prosper. So why be stagnant if you can keep learning?

Regardless of your academic background, if, for example, you completed high school, or took a technical or higher education course, don't just settle down for what you learned in formal education. There is a lot of knowledge available you can use to improve the skills and abilities you going to need in your professional life.

And why is this so important? You know when you feel like you've done a good job, but you don't feel rewarded for it? Sometimes the problem is that we have a wrong perception of our work. It may even seem like we've done something great, but that only happened in our head, because we're limited to what we can understand at that moment. You may think that was an amazing work, but it truly wasn't.

So, it is important that you know what you need and how you can obtain knowledge, as this will give you greater power over your career.

List what you need. For example, do you lack computer

skills? Do you need to improve your English? What other technical things do you need to know about? Make a list and **prioritize** what you want to learn this year. Try to use as many free tools as you can. There is a lot of knowledge available on YouTube, blogs, Facebook pages, LinkedIn, etc. Look for cheaper, short-term options before embarking on more extensive courses. If you take long-term courses without having given it too much thought, it will be easier to **regret** it halfway through.

If you're interested in a specific area, try short courses on that subject to see if you really want to go further. There are courses for everything you can imagine at very affordable prices. These days it's much easier to find exactly what you need to fill a specific gap.

Also, look for knowledge in books and magazines related to your profession. Talk to other professionals in the field. Always try to feed the flame of **curiosity**, even if you are interested in something that seems to have nothing to do with your work at the moment. Understand that all knowledge is valid because it helps us to give our brain a boost.

Next, we're going to do a little exercise on what we've seen in this section. And then, we will see how to combine

activities and **learning**.

Task: What do you need to learn?

List the skills, abilities and other knowledge that can help you advance in your career.

Examples:

- Write and edit texts in Microsoft Word.

- Build spreadsheets in Microsoft Excel.

- Create impactful presentations in Microsoft Power Point.

- Learn to speak in public.

- Edit images in Adobe Photoshop.

- Learn to program in HTML5.

***

After creating your list, select the items you consider **most important** at the moment and plan to gain this knowledge in the coming months. Resist the temptation to do everything at once, focus on just **one** or **two** items of the list.

Combining activities and learning

It is normal to think we must separate a time for study and a time for leisure. But thinking like that only drives us further away from studies out of sheer laziness to start. Our brain doesn't want to work; it just wants to have fun. That's why it's so hard to sit down and study. You will think of every possible and imaginable excuse to delay your studies. Whether checking out your cell phone, browsing on Facebook, watching a video on YouTube. So, since we know this happens, how about we make the most of this situation?

Imagine you've committed to learn another language, but you can't concentrate to study by a book. At the same time, there's a movie you're really want to watch. Well, if the original language of this movie is the same you're learning, how about watching it with subtitles, instead of dubbed in English? That way, you will do something you enjoy and you can also exercise a skill.

Another example: if you have a technical subject to learn and you also need to study another language, then how about getting a book on the subject in the language you need to practice?

And don't think that it boils down to studying another language. Imagine you are doing some chore around the house like cooking, washing dishes or doing laundry. How about playing a **video** lesson at your cell phone in the meantime? Or, if you take the bus or subway, you could buy **audiobooks** to listen along the way. Or even listen to **podcasts** about your area of interest while doing your workout, for example.

There is not just one way to learn something. If you're trying to study by reading a book and it's not working, try to find another way to learn that subject. Not all people learn the same way. Make your learning **fun**. If you're bored, you're probably not retaining anything you're trying to learn.

And finally, strive to learn something new **every day**. It doesn't even have to be anything big. After all, small daily doses of knowledge are enough to keep your brain fed and happy.

Summing up

In this chapter, we looked at how you can find out if you are happy with your current **profession** and what you can do if you want to change careers. We have seen that learning is an **ongoing** process and you will need to continue studying and **improving** yourself even if you already have a doctorate degree, for example.

And finally, we saw that it is possible to combine **daily activities** with **learning**.

CONCLUSION

Congratulations on getting here!

You may have noticed this book is short, but it gets right to the point. I sincerely hope that you can apply these tips in your daily life.

If you've been procrastinating a lot on your tasks and projects, remember all you have to do is put your anxiety aside and **get started**, even if you get a bad start. It may seem like easier said than done, but give it a try. You can always review what you've done, but you won't be able to review something you didn't even start.

Get in the habit of organizing your **schedule** weekly, leaving the most **complex** tasks to be done at the beginning of the day. And remember to always leave free time in case you need to deal with unforeseen.

Assess whether the means of **communication** you are using are the most appropriate for each situation. Beware of English mistakes, defensiveness posture and gossip at work. Always seek to be interested in what people are saying, really observe and listen to them.

When faced with problems, try to know as much as possible about them and strive to be a **Problem Solver**, that is, the person who is there to solve and not to complicate the situation.

Also remember that the more we learn, the more we have the capacity to learn.

Don't create limitations for yourself, after all, you can be much more than you are today.

FINAL WORDS

If you liked this book, please write a review at Amazon. It's pretty quick. I really hope you have a lot of success in your career!

Follow the author at: @milakinoinsta

By the way, did you know that I also write fiction? :)

The Guest

If you like psychological horror stories, this one is for you. After hours traveling through the night, Dennis has finally found a place to rest his bones from him... But the Golden Hotel hides a

 terrible secret.